MOUNTAIN OF FIRE AND MIRACLES MINISTRIES

13, Olasimbo Street, off Olumo Road,
Onike P. O. Box 2990, Sabo, Yaba, Lagos.

PRAY
Your Way
into
2016

The Mountain of Fire and Miracles Ministries, is a ministry devoted to the Revival of Apostolic Signs, Holy Ghost Fireworks and the Unlimited Demonstration of the Power of God to deliver to the uttermost.

At MFM all over the world, holiness within and without, as the greatest spiritual insecticide and a condition for heaven, is being taught openly, MFM is a do-it-yourself gospel ministry. There, your hands are trained to war and your fingers to fight.

If you are in Lagos, join us at the International Headquarters, 13 Olasimbo Street, off Olumo Road, Onike, Yaba, or any of our branches worldwide (www.mountainoffire.org) and see the manifestation of the power of God that answers by fire in promoting you and demoting your adversaries.

God bless you richly as you enter the new year with the power of new beginning.

MEETING DAYS AT THE INTERNATIONAL HEADQUARTERS

Day	Service	Time
Sunday	Worship Service	7:00 am
Monday	Spiritual Hospital	5:00 pm
Wednesday	MFM Revival Service	5:00 pm
1st Saturday	Power Must Change Hands	7:00 am (at Prayer City)

Day 1

RUN THROUGH THE TROOPS

Scripture Reading: Psalm 18

Confession: 1 John 4:4

Hymn

1. Now thank we all our God
   With heart and hands and voices,
   Who wondrous things hath done,
   In whom His world rejoices;
   Who, from our mother's arms,
   Hath blest us on our way
   With countless gifts of love,
   And still is ours today.

2. O may this bounteous God
   Through all our life be nears us,
   With ever joyful hearts
   And blessed peace to cheer us;
   And keep us in His grace,
   And guide us when perplexed,
   And free us from all ills
   In this world and the next.

3. All praise and thanks to God
   The Father now be given
   The Son, and Him who reigns
   With them in highest heaven,
   The one eternal God,
   Whom earth and heav'n adore,
   For thus it was, is now,
   And shall be evermore.

Praise and Worship

1. Thank God for making every evil arrow fired against your life to back fire.

2. Thank God for disengaging the satanic network fashioned against your life in the second heaven and on earth.

3. Every organised battle against my life, scatter, in Jesus' name.

4. Any power using my name and picture for evil purposes, scatter, in Jesus' name.

5. Every foundation of witchcraft in my family line, die, in Jesus' name.
6. I shall not be demoted, I shall go from glory to glory, in Jesus' name.
7. Every spiritual funeral procession organised against me, scatter, in Jesus' name.
8. Every enchantment assigned against me, die, in Jesus' name.
9. Every witchcraft agenda for my life, die, in Jesus' name.
10. Every embargo of darkness on my glory, die, in Jesus' name.
11. Every problem designed to destroy my destiny, die, in Jesus' name.
12. Violently, forcefully, I take back everything the enemy has stolen from me, in Jesus' name.
13. Every plan and assignment of the strongman, die, in Jesus' name.
14. My Father, let me become pure terror and dread to the enemies, in Jesus' name.

Now, make these confessions out loud

1. No counsel of the wicked shall stand against me, in the name of Jesus.
2. Unto me, shall God do exceeding abundantly above all that I ask, seek, desire and think, according to the power that He had made to work in me, in the name of Jesus.
3. As it is written, I shall be a crown of glory in the hand of God, a royal diadem in the hand of my Maker. I begin to shine as a shining light. The light of God is in me.
4. The word of God has made me a brazen wall, a fortified city, an iron pillar, therefore presence terrifies the enemy. He trembles, feels much pain and travails at the sound of my voice which the Lord has empowered. For it is written, wherever the voice of the king is, there is authority.
5. My appearance is as the appearance of a horse. So, I leap, I run like mighty men. When I fall upon the sword, it cannot hurt me, in the name of Jesus.
6. God has equipped me and made me a danger and a terror to all my enemies, in the name of Jesus.
7. The Lord is my light and my salvation, whom shall I fear? The Lord is the strength of my life; of whom shall I be afraid? When the wicked, even mine enemies and my foes, came upon me to eat up my flesh, they stumbled and fell, in the name of Jesus.

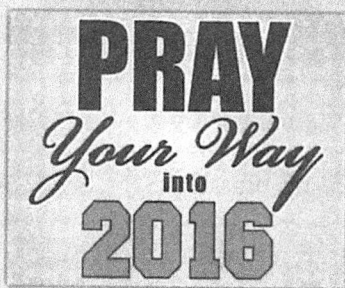

Scripture Reading: Psalm 150

Confession: Isaiah 61:3

Hymn

1. They were gathered in an upper chamber,
   As commanded by the risen Lord,
   And the promise of the Father
   There they sought with one accord,
   When the Holy Ghost from heaven descended
   Like a rushing wind and tongues of fire:
   So dear Lord, we seek Thy blessing,
   Come with glory now our hearts inspire.

   Let the fire fall, let the fire fall,
   Let the fire from heaven fall;
   We are waiting and expecting,
   Now in faith, dear Lord, we call;
   Let the fire fall, let the fire fall,
   On Thy promise we depend;
   From the glory of Thy presence
   Let the Pentecostal fire descend.

2. As Elijah we would raise the altar
   For our testimony clear and true,
   Christ the Saviour, loving Healer,
   Coming Lord, Baptizer too,
   Ever flowing grace and full salvation,
   For a ruined race Thy love has planned;
   For this blessed revelation,
   For Thy written word we dare to stand.

3. 'Tis the covenanted promise given
   To as many as the Lord shall call,
   To the fathers and their children,
   To Thy people, one and all;
   So rejoicing in Thy word unfailing,
   We draw nigh in faith Thy power to know
   Come, O come, Thou burning Spirit,
   Set our hearts with heavenly fire aglow.

4. With a living coal from off Thy altar
   Touch our lips to swell Thy wondrous praise,
   To extol Thee, bless, adore Thee,
   And our songs of worship raise;
   Let the cloud of glory now descending
   Fill our hearts with holy ecstasy,
   Come in all Thy glorious fullness,
   Blessed Holy Spirit, have Thy way.

Praise and Worship

1. Thank God for making your Haman to die instead of you.
2. Thank God for the eyes that do not sleep nor slumber that watch over you day and night.
3. I move from the territory of disgrace into the arena of elevation, in Jesus' name.

4. I swim from the river of pain into the river of gain, in the name of Jesus.

5. I fly from the sky of rejection to the firmament of dominion, in Jesus' name.

6. I move away from the bus stop of stagnancy to accelerated breakthroughs, in the name of Jesus.

7. Every limitation imposed by darkness upon my breakthroughs, break, in the name of Jesus.

8. Every power dispatched from hell to frustrate me, scatter, in the name of Jesus.

9. Fire of God, arise, swallow every darkness in my life, in the name of Jesus.

10. Every plantation of darkness in my life, die, by the power in the blood of Jesus.

11. Every poison in my body, die, in the name of Jesus.

12. Every negative atmosphere around me, scatter, in the name of Jesus.

13. Any rope tying me down to the same spot, break, in the name of Jesus.

14. Every witchcraft war from my foundation, die, in the name of Jesus.

Now, make these confessions out loud

1. I totally trust in the Lord, and I am not leaning on my own understanding. I fill my heart with the words of faith; I receive and speak the words of faith.

2. The young lions do lack, and suffer hunger; but I who seek the Lord God Almighty, shall not lack any good thing, in the name of Jesus.

3. God is my strong Rock and my house of defence, in the name of Jesus.

4. In the name of Jesus Christ, I handover all my battles to the Lord Jesus Christ, He fights for me and I hold my peace.

5. The Lord has bowed down His righteous ears to deliver me speedily, in the name of Jesus.

6. I shall eat the riches of the Gentiles, in their glory I shall boast myself; all shall see and shall acknowledge that I am the seed, which the Lord has blessed.

7. I shall no longer be disappointed, or fail at the edge of my desired miracles, success and victory, in the name of Jesus.

PRAY
Your Way
into
2016

Day **3**

December 26 2015

FROM INSULT
TO RESULT

Scripture Reading: 1 Samuel 1
Confession: Isaiah 12:3
Hymn

1. God sent His Son, they called Him Jesus;
   He came to love, heal and forgive;
   He lived and died to buy my pardon,
   An empty grave is there to prove my Saviour lives

   Because He lives I can face tomorrow;
   Because He lives all fear is gone;
   Because I know He holds the future,
   And life is worth the living just because He lives

2. How sweet to hold a new born baby,
   And feel the pride and joy he gives;
   But greater still the calm assurance,
   This child can face uncertain days because He lives

3. And then one day I'll cross the river;
   I'll fight life's final war with pain;
   And then as death gives way to vict'ry,
   I'll see the lights of glory and I'll know He lives

Praise and Worship

1. Thank God for disallowing evil testimonies over your life and family.
2. Thank God for empowering you to defeat the Goliath of your life.
3. Every power waging war against my destiny, fall down and die, in Jesus' name.
4. I overthrow every satanic rearrangement programmed against my destiny, in the name of Jesus.
5. I refuse to accept satanic substitute for my destiny, in Jesus' name.
6. Every power drawing powers from the heavenlies against my destiny, fall down and die, in Jesus' name.
7. Today, I raise an altar of continuous prosperity upon my destiny, in Jesus' name
8. I reject every satanic rearrangement of my destiny, in Jesus' name.

9. I reject and renounce destiny-demoting names and I nullify their evil effects upon my destiny, in Jesus' name.

10. The designs of my enemy against my destiny shall be destroyed, in Jesus' name.

11. Conspiracy of darkness against my destiny, scatter by fire, in the name of Jesus.

12. You evil strongman attached to my destiny, be bound, in Jesus' name.

13. Every evil against me, be judged today, in the name of Jesus.

14. Every power assigned to put ashes on my head, die, in the name of Jesus.

Now, make these confessions out loud

1. The Spirit of life in Christ Jesus that dwells inside me, has delivered me from the law of sin and death including satan, in the name of Jesus.

2. I know by the word of God that, there are many devices in a man's heart; nevertheless it is the counsel of the Lord that shall stand in my life, in the name of Jesus.

3. Jehovah God is all-sufficient and He is more than sufficient. I ask for God's divine abundance in every area of my life and I receive it by faith, in the name of Jesus.

4. I receive unto myself, the virtues, the strength, the power, the might and the anointing in the blood of Jesus. And I say, let the blood quicken all that is dead within me. If the enemy comes against me, the Spirit of the Lord will lift up a standard against them and they cannot pass through, in Jesus' name.

5. No one, whether they be principalities, powers, dominions, all of the powers of darkness and even satan himself, can pluck me out of the mighty hand of God; for my God is stronger than all, in Jesus' name.

6. The Lord will make His face to shine upon me always, and shall be gracious unto me. His light will shine on my path and His favour will encompass me all the days of my life.

7. No weapon that is fashioned against me shall prosper, and every tongue that rises up against me is already condemned, in the name of Jesus.

PRAY
Your Way
into
2016

Day**4**

December 27 2015

MY PROBLEM SHALL BECOME PROMOTION

Scripture Reading: 1 Samuel 17

Confession: Psalm 18:37

Hymn

1. Let us with a gladsome mind,
   Praise the Lord for He is kind:
   For His mercies ay endure,
   Ever faithful, ever sure.

2. Let us blaze His name abroad,
   For of gods He is the God:
   For His mercies ay endure,
   Ever faithful, ever sure.

3. He with all commanding might
   Filled the new made world with light:
   For His mercies ay endure,
   Ever faithful, ever sure.

4. He the golden tressed sun
   Caused all day His course to run:
   For His mercies ay endure,
   Ever faithful, ever sure.

5. And the horned moon at night
   'Mid her spangled sisters bright:
   For His mercies ay endure,
   Ever faithful, ever sure.

6. All things living He doth feed,
   His full hand supplies their need:
   For His mercies ay endure,
   Ever faithful, ever sure.

Praise and Worship

1. Thank God for disallowing evil testimonies over your life and family.

2. Thank God for empowering you to defeat the Goliath of your life.

3. Any evil power claiming right to my breakthroughs, fall down and die, in the name of Jesus.

4. Any power from the pit of hell killing my breakthroughs, be devoured by the Lion of Judah, in the name of Jesus.

5. I release the blood of Jesus into my career, in the name of Jesus.

6. Every spirit of the tail tying me down in the valley of poverty, die, in the name of Jesus.

7. Every foundational poverty of my father's house, my destiny is not your candidate, release me and die, in the name of Jesus.

8. Every circle of hardship in my foundation, release me and die, in the name of Jesus.

9. Every blockage working against my breakthroughs, scatter, in the name of Jesus.

10. I withdraw my name from the book of failure, in the name of Jesus.

11. I withdraw my name from the book of poverty, in the name of Jesus.

12. Every evil power discouraging my helper, lose your power, in the name of Jesus.

13. I refuse to be a beggar in the market of life, in the name of Jesus.

14. By fire, by thunder, I possess all my possession in the warehouse of satan, in the name of Jesus.

Now, make these confessions out loud

1. I can do and possess all things, through Christ who strengthens me. And my God shall supply all my needs according to His riches in glory by Christ Jesus.

2. My heart is from now comforted, for the God of suddenly, provision and grace is still on the throne, in the name of Jesus.

3. I trust in the Word of God, the Word stands sure, when I speak it, it will accomplish the purpose for which I have spoken it, in Jesus' name.

4. I am the manifestation, the product and the result of God's word. God has spoken into my life and I have become the manifest presence of Jehovah God on earth. I expressly manifest everything, the word of God says I am. I am filled with the word of life.

5. Because the Lord disappointeth the devices of the crafty, so that their hands cannot perform their enterprise. Every work of the strong, the wicked, the evil and the enemy against my life, shall not prosper, in the name of Jesus.

6. I claim the power in the name of the Lord to overcome all the troops of the enemy, in the name of Jesus.

7. In the name of Jesus Christ, by the presence of God in my life, I command the wicked to perish before me; and melt away like wax in the fire.

I SHALL MOUNT UP LIKE EAGLES

Scripture Reading: Romans 8
Confession: Isaiah 40:31
Hymn

1. The God of Abra'am praise
Who reigns enthroned above;
Ancient of everlasting days,
And God of love; Jehovah, Great I AM,
By earth and heaven confess'd
I bow and bless the sacred name
For ever bless'd.

2. The God of Abra'am praise
At whose supreme command
From earth I rise, and seek the joys
At His right hand: I all on earth forsake
Its wisdom, fame, and power;
And Him my only portion make,
My shield and tower

3. He by Himself hath sworn;
I on His oath depend;
I shall, on eagle's wings upborne,
To heaven ascend; I shall behold His face,
I shall His power adore;
And sing the wonders of His grace
For evermore.

4. Though nature's strength decay,
And earth and hell withstand,
To Canaan's bounds I urge my way,
At His command The watery deep I pass,
With Jesus in my view;
And through the howling wilderness
My way pursue.

5. The God, who reigns on high,
The great archangels sing,
And "Holy, Holy, Holy' cry
Almighty King; Who was and is the same
And evermore shall be:
Jehovah, Father, Great I AM,
We worship Thee.

6. The whole triumphant host
Give thanks to God on high;
Hail, Father, Son and Holy Ghost,
They ever cry. Hail, Abra'am's God, and mine,
I join the heavenly lays;
All might and majesty are Thine,
And endless praise.

Praise and Worship

1. O God, I thank You for You are kind to me when I've been put to shame.
2. O God, I thank You for turning me into an overcomer.
3. Blood of Jesus, laminate my life, in the name of Jesus.
4. I tread upon every serpent of poverty assigned against my life, in the name of Jesus.
5. Any power assigned to kill me, kill yourself, in the name of Jesus.

6. Arise O God and let my environment be sanitised for dominion prosperity, in the name of Jesus.

7. Every garment of sorrow prepared for my life, catch fire, in the name of Jesus.

8. Any power on any assignment to waste my life, fall down and die, in Jesus' name.

9. Any power assigned to toy with my destiny, scatter, in the name of Jesus.

10. Let the labours of my enemy receive double failure, in the name of Jesus.

11. Every circumstance threatening to disrupt my life, die, in the name of Jesus.

12. Every evil call, assigned against my life, back fire, in the name of Jesus.

13. The miracle that will make me a candidate of supernatural surprises, locate my life by fire, in the name of Jesus.

14. O God, arise and let my past losses be restored seven-fold, in Jesus' name.

Now, make these confessions out loud

1. The word of God says that He will restore to me the years that the locust, the cankerworm, and the caterpillar, and the palmerworm have eaten, in the name of Jesus.

2. With the blood of Jesus, the Lord will flush my land and wash my palms and possessions, in the name of Jesus.

3. The whole world may decide to go wild with evil flowing like a flood. The enemy, in his evil machinations, may decide against me. The earth may choose not to tremble; whatever may be or happen, I refuse to be shaken, in the name of Jesus.

4. Who is like unto the Lord, our God, who dwells on high, far above all powers and dominions? He raiseth up the poor out of the dust, and lifteth the needy out of the dunghill; that He might set him with princes. Even so shall the Lord deal with me, in the name of Jesus.

5. The Bible says that whatsoever I desire when I pray, I should believe and receive, in the name of Jesus. Therefore, I pray now that, in Jesus' name, I am set free from every captivity or attack of negative speech from my mouth or thoughts and from my heart, against myself.

6. I tear down, in faith, every spiritual wall of partition, between me and my divinely appointed helpers and benefactors, in the name of Jesus.

7. It is written, "If God be for us, who can be against us?" God is with me; I have no reason to fear, in the name of Jesus.

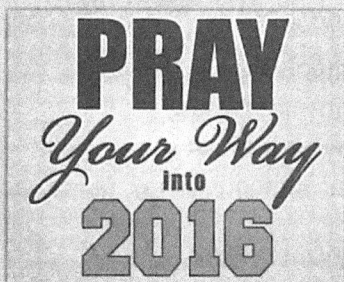

Scripture Reading: Esther 2
Confession: Psalm 27:6
Hymn

1.   Holy, holy, holy, Lord God Almighty
     Early in the morning our song shall rise to Thee
     Holy, holy, holy, merciful and mighty!
     God in three Persons, blessed Trinity.

2.   Holy, holy, holy, all the saints adore Thee,
     Casting down their golden crowns around the glassy sea
     Cherubim and Seraphim falling down before
     Thee, Which wert and art and evermore shall be.

3.   Holy, holy, holy, though the darkness hide Thee,
     Though the eye of sinful man Thy glory may not see;
     Only Thou art holy, there is none beside Thee,
     Perfect in pow'r, in love and purity.

4.   Holy, holy, holy, Lord God Almighty!
     All Thy works shall praise Thy name in earth and sky and sea
     Holy, holy, holy! Merciful and mighty!,
     God in three Persons, blessed Trinity!

Praise and Worship

1.   Father, I praise You for being my Hiding Place.
2.   Father, I thank You for being my Defender.
3.   Let the teeth of the enemy over my life break, in the name of Jesus.
4.   Every ancient gate of my place of birth, locking up my progress, hear the word of the Lord, lift your heads and open, in the name of Jesus.
5.   My glory, what are you doing in the valley? Arise and shine, in the name of Jesus.

6. Let every covenant with the sun, moon and stars against my life be broken, in the name of Jesus.

7. I shall not be a spiritual casualty, in the name of Jesus.

8. I break the law of death over my life, in the name of Jesus.

9. I am invisible to aggressive elements, in the name of Jesus.

10. Every evil power that has established authority in my family, be dismantled, in the name of the Jesus.

11. I pull down every throne of iniquity, in the name of Jesus.

12. My portion is not with the dead, in the name of Jesus.

13. I quench every anger energised through the land against me, in the name of Jesus.

14. Every conglomeration of witches, be melted, in the name of Jesus.

Now, make these confessions out loud

1. Every curse of death, poverty, lust or every vagabond anointing issued by occultist, witches, rulers of darkness and local wickedness against me, a God's anointed, shall not prosper.

2. My heart shall thrill with joy and be enlarged, because the abundance of the sea shall be turned to me, in the name of Jesus.

3. Foreigners shall build up walls for me and their kings shall minister unto me, in the name of Jesus.

4. Every dry bone in my life, shall God raise with the fullness of His eternal, abundant life, in the name of Jesus.

5. The great army of God is beside me. I shall eat in plenty and be satisfied, and praise the name of the Lord my God, who hath dealt wondrously with me, and I shall never be ashamed.

6. The devil has no more dominion over me, in the name of Jesus

7. Surely, there is no enchantment against me, neither is there any divination against me, in the name of Jesus.

PRAY
Your Way Into 2016

WHO ART THOU GREAT MOUNTAIN?

Scripture Reading: John 11

Confession: Psalm 118:17

Hymn

1. Praise, my soul, the King of heaven,
   To His feet thy tribute bring;
   Ransomed, healed, restored, forgiven,
   Who like the His praise shall sing;
   Praise Him, Praise Him,
   Praise the everlasting King.

2. Praise Him for His grace and favour
   To our fathers in distress;
   Praise Him, still the same for ever,
   Slow to chide, and swift to bless;
   Praise Him, Praise Him,
   Glorious in His faithfulness.

3. Father like, He tends and spares us;
   Well our feeble frame He knows;
   In His hands He gently bears us,
   Rescues us from all our foes;
   Praise Him, Praise Him,
   Widely as His mercy flows.

4. Angels in the height, adore Him;
   Ye behold Him face to face;
   Sun and moon, bow down before Him;
   Dwellers all in time and space;
   Praise Him, Praise Him,
   Praise with us the God of grace

Praise and Worship

1. Lord, I give You praise for delivering my soul from death and my feet from stumbling.

2. Oh God, I thank You because You will be my guide even to the end.

3. Every complicated evil network against me, be eaten up by the elements, in the name of Jesus.

4. The evil mystery against me, collapse and fail, in the name of Jesus.

5. Committee of demons who sat on my case, I reconvene your meeting, I cancel your decision and I bring the judgement of God against you, in the name of Jesus.

6. Every evil altar, be swallowed, in the name of Jesus.

7. Household witchcraft, I melt your power, in the name of Jesus.

8. Every pot cooking my affairs, the Lord rebuke you, in the name of Jesus.

9. I break the spell of any witchcraft pot from my neck, in the name of Jesus.

10. I break every witchcraft pot over my life, in the name of Jesus.

11. Let every pot hunt its owners, in the name of Jesus.

12. Every ancient pot of my father's house, I am not your victim, catch fire, in the name of Jesus.

13. You troublers of my Israel, God has ordained me as a god over you, I command you to bow, in the name of Jesus.

14. Every mystery of hell over my life, I command you to break, in the name of Jesus.

Now, make these confessions out loud

1. I receive the blood of Jesus Christ upon me and upon my house where I live, in the name of Jesus.

2. I conquer and I lock my enemies all up, for God is for me and no one can rise up or be against me, in the name of Jesus.

3. Because the Lord disappointeth the devices of the crafty, so that their hands cannot perform their enterprise, every work of the strong, the wicked, the evil and the enemy against my life, shall not prosper, in the name of Jesus.

4. If the enemy comes against me, the Spirit of the Lord will lift up a standard against them and they cannot pass through, in Jesus' name.

5. Speedily the Lord will hear me, and speedily will He deliver me from the curse of my lack and unfruitfulness, in the name of Jesus

6. I receive unto myself, the virtues, the strength, the power, the might and the anointing in the blood of Jesus. And I say, let the blood quicken all that is dead within me.

7. The daughters of those who afflicted me shall come bending low to me, and all those who hated me shall bow down at my feet.

NEW YEAR PROGRAMME

Hymn No. 1 King of Glory, King of Peace

1. King of glory, King of peace,
   I will love Thee;
   And that love may never cease,
   I will move Thee
   Thou hast granted my request,
   Thou hast heard me;
   Thou didst note my working breast,
   Thou hast spare me.

2. Wherefore with my utmost art
   I will sing Thee,
   And the cream of all my heart
   I will bring Thee.
   Though my sins against me cried,
   Thou didst clear me,
   And alone, when they replied,
   Thou didst hear me.

3. Seven whole days, not one in seven,
   I will praise Thee;
   In my heart, though not in heaven,
   I can raise Thee.
   Small it is, in this poor sort
   To enrol Thee;
   E'en eternity's too short
   To extol Thee.

Hymn No. 2

1. All creatures of our God and King
   Lift up your voice and with us sing,
   Alleluia! Alleluia!
   Thou burning sun with golden beam,
   Thou silver moon with softer gleam!

   O praise Him! O praise Him!
   Alleluia! Alleluia! Alleluia!

2. Thou rushing wind that art so strong
   Ye clouds that sail in Heaven along,
   O praise Him! Alleluia!
   Thou rising morn, in praise rejoice,
   Ye lights of evening, find a voice!

3. Thou flowing water, pure and clear,
   Make music for thy Lord to hear,
   O praise Him! Alleluia!
   Thou fire so masterful and bright,
   That givest man both warmth and light.

4. Dear mother earth, who day by day
   Unfoldest blessings on our way,
   O praise Him! Alleluia!
   The flowers and fruits that in thee grow,
   Let them His glory also show.

5. And all ye men of tender heart,
   Forgiving others, take your part,
   O sing ye! Alleluia!
   Ye who long pain and sorrow bear,
   Praise God and on Him cast your care.

6. And thou most kind and gentle Death,
   Waiting to hush our latest breath,
   O praise Him! Alleluia!
   Thou leadest home the child of God,
   And Christ our Lord the way hath trod.

7. Let all things their Creator bless,
   And worship Him in humbleness,
   O praise Him! Alleluia!
   Praise, praise the Father, praise the Son,
   And praise the Spirit, Three in One!

Hymn No. 3

1. O God, our help in ages past,
   Our hope for years to come,
   Our shelter from the stormy blast,
   And our eternal home.

2. Under the shadow of Thy throne
   Thy saints have dwelt secure;
   Sufficient is Thine arm alone,
   And our defence is sure.

3. Before the hills in order stood,
   Or earth received her frame,
   From everlasting Thou art God,
   To endless years the same.

4. A thousand ages in Thy sight
   Are like an evening gone;
   Short as the watch that ends the night
   Before the rising sun.

5. Time, like an ever-rolling stream,
   Bears all its sons away;
   They fly forgotten, as a dream
   Dies at the opening day.

6. O God, our help in ages past,
   Our hope for years to come,
   Be Thou our guard while life shall last
   And our eternal home.

2016 PROSPERITY PRAYER POINTS

Jesus is Lord of this earth. The earth with all its fullness belongs to God. As a joint heir with Jesus, I claim the wealth of this earth, for it belongs to Jesus. I claim all that Jesus' death made available for me to receive. In Jesus' name, I command you devil to lose the wealth of this earth! Take your hands off now! I command every hindering force to stop! In Jesus' name, I bind you and render you ineffective against me! In Jesus' name, I command wealth to come to me now! Jesus is Lord of my life. Jesus is Lord of my finances. Jesus is Lord!

The Lord is my banker; I shall not owe. He maketh me to lie down in green pastures; He restoreth my loss: He leadeth me beside still waters. Yea though I walk in the valley of the shadow of debt, I will fear no evil, for thou art with me; thy silver and thy gold, they rescue me. Thou preparest a way for me in the presence of business competitors; Thou anointed my head with oil, my cup runneth over. Surely goodness and mercy shall follow me all the days of my life and I shall do business in the name of the Lord. Amen

As God was with Joseph in Potiphar's house and business, so the Lord is with me. As things prospered in Joseph's hand, so all that I lay my hands upon shall prosper. I will be blessed at home and I will be blessed in my fields.

My God has enough riches in heaven in Christ Jesus. I enter into this from now on, in Jesus' name.

I have passed through the night of financial crisis. My morning of joy is coming beginning from today.

I delight myself in the Word of the Lord, therefore, I am blessed. Wealth and riches shall be in my house and my righteousness endureth forever. (Ps 112:1-3.)

I remember the Lord my God, for it is He that giveth me power to get wealth. (Deut. 8:18.)

With me are riches and honour, enduring wealth and prosperity. (Prov. 8:18.)

I am crowned with wealth. (Prov. 14:24.)

I know the grace of my Lord Jesus Christ, that, though He was rich, yet for my sakes He became poor, that through His poverty I might be rich. (2 Corn. 8:9.)

I shout for joy: Let the Lord be magnified, which hath pleasure in the prosperity of His servant. (Psalm 35:27.)

The Lord is my shepherd. (Psalm 23:1.)

The Lord prepares a table before me in the presence of my enemies, He anoints my head with oil, my cup runneth over. (Psalm 23:5.)

The blessing of the Lord makes me rich and He adds no trouble to it. (Prov. 10:22.)

I receive wealth from the Lord and the good health to enjoy it. (Eccl. 5:19.)

I am blessed because I trust in the Lord. I reverence the Lord, therefore is no want in my life. The young lions do lack and suffer hunger: But I shall not want any good thing. (Psalm 34:8-10.)

I have given and it shall be given unto me, good measure, pressed down, shaken together and running over, shall men give into my bosom. For with the same measure that I mete withal it shall be measured to me again. (Luke 6:38.)

God is able to make all grace abound toward me, that I, always having all sufficiency in all things, may have an abundance for every good work. (2 Corn. 9:8.)

I am prospering in every way. My body keeps well, even as my soul keeps well and prosper. (3 John 2.)

Whatsoever I ask the Father in the name of His Son Jesus, He will give it to me. (John 16:23.)

Abraham's blessings are mine. (Gal. 3:14.)

What things soever I desire, when I pray, I believe that I have received them and I shall have them. (Mark 11:24.)

I delight myself in the Lord, and He gives me the desires of my heart. (Psalm 37:4.)

I seek first the kingdom of God, therefore everything I need shall be added unto me. (Lk. 12:31.)

The wealth of the sinner is laid up for me. (Prov. 13:22.)

My inheritance shall be forever. I shall not be ashamed in the evil time: and in the days of famine I shall be satisfied. (Psalm 37:18-19.)

Every burden shall be taken away from off my shoulder, and every yoke from off my neck, and the yoke shall be destroyed because of the anointing. (Isa. 10:27.)

I am like a tree that's planted by the rivers of water. Everything I do shall prosper. (Psalm 1:3.)

I will not faint, for in due time and at the appointed season I shall reap, if I faint not. (Gal. 6:9.)

My God supplies all of my needs according to His riches in glory by Christ Jesus. (Phil. 4:19.)

There will be no poverty of body, soul and spirit in my life. The anointing of God upon my life gives me favour in the eyes of God and man all the days of my life. I shall not labour in vain. I shall walk this day in victory and liberty of the spirit.

I bind all evil spirits in me or that are attacking me, in the name of Jesus.

Anything from the kingdom of darkness that has made it its business to hinder me, I single you out right now, and bind you with chains that cannot be broken, in the name of Jesus; I strip off all your spiritual armour, in the name of Jesus. I command you to lose the support of other evil powers, in the name of Jesus. I command you not to involve yourself with me again, in the name of Jesus.

Aggressive Praise and Worship

1. O heavens over my prosperity, open by fire, in the name of Jesus.

2. O God, arise and empower me to prosper, in the name of Jesus.

3. Every power seating on my wealth, fall down and die, in the name of Jesus.

4. Foundational poverty, die, in the name of Jesus.

5. I take authority over and order the binding of the strongman of financial failure, in the name of Jesus.

6. I break every covenant of poverty of my father's house, in the name of Jesus.

7. I enter into the covenant of prosperity and abundance with the Elshadai, in Jesus' name.

8. Every curse and covenant responsible for financial mess, I revoke you, in the name of Jesus.

9. Every evil power, that will contest my voice this year, be silenced, in Jesus' name.

10. Every power that will contend with my divine destiny this year, scatter, in Jesus' name.

11. Oh star of my destiny, arise and shine this year, in the name of Jesus.

12. I silence every strange altar sacrificing my divine opportunities, in Jesus' name.

13. Blood of Jesus, wipe off all handwriting of failure in my life.

14. Every tree of bad luck, be uprooted by fire, in the name of Jesus.

15. Fire of God, deal with every root of misfortune, in the name of Jesus.

16. When and where others are confused, I shall succeed, I shall get maximum profit, in Jesus' name.

17. O God, arise and teach me how to profit, in the name of Jesus.

18. O God, arise and teach me how to produce wealth, even in a bad economy, in the name of Jesus.

19. My Father, breathe upon all I will do this year, in the name of Jesus.

20. Every strongman of failure at the edge of my breakthrough die, in Jesus' name.

21. Blood of Jesus, dissolve the root of disgrace, in the name of Jesus.

22. Every witchcraft altar, raised against my breakthrough, die, in Jesus' name.

23. Every ancestral debt-collector forcing me to pay for what I did not buy, die, in the name of Jesus.

24. I reject the life of survival on debt. I receive financial breakthroughs to clear the debts, in the name of Jesus.

25. Thou power of family curse and covenant of poverty over my life, break, in the name of Jesus.

26. Those that despise me in the past shall see my favour, in the name of Jesus.

27. Those who belittle me shall witness my progress, in the name of Jesus.

28. Every cycle of backwardness, break, in the name of Jesus.

29. Prosperity famine, die, in the name of Jesus.

30. Every seed of failure planted in my family line, die, in the name of Jesus.

31. Thou power of aimlessness, die, in the name of Jesus.

32. Lord, anoint my brain to prosper after the order of Bazaleel, the son of Uri, the son of Hui, of the tribe of Judah, in the name of Jesus.

33. I ask for the release of prosperity on my life, in the name of Jesus.

34. Let all demonic hindrances to my finances be totally paralysed, in Jesus' name.

35. Fire of God, roast all witchcraft bags holding my breakthrough, in Jesus' name.

36. Every spiritual satanic bank manager, die, in the name of Jesus.

37. Every dark hand in my foundation, waging war against my destiny, wither, in the name of Jesus.

38. Let men go out of their ways to show favour unto me, in the name of Jesus.

39. Lord, let not the lot of the wicked fall upon my life, in the name of Jesus.
40. Every satanic investigation into my future, be dismantled, in Jesus' name.
41. O Lord, give me the achievement that will swallow past failure, in Jesus' name.
42. Every weapon of shame directed against my life, lose your power, in Jesus' name.
43. Every satanic arrow, fired against my star, fall down and die, in Jesus' name.
44. My destiny, jump out of debt, in the name of Jesus.
45. Every enemy of my progress, scatter, in the name of Jesus.
46. Every enemy of my miracles, scatter, in the name of Jesus.
47. Thou power of the earth, release my buried virtue, in the name of Jesus.
48. Thou power in the heavenlies, release my captured star, in Jesus' name.
49. My destiny, reject witchcraft foundation, in the name of Jesus.
50. O Lord, shake down every foundation of hardship, in the name of Jesus.
51. Every blessing, that has passed me by, be returned, in the name of Jesus.
52. Every demonic rat in my prosperity, die, in the name of Jesus.
53. Fire of God, melt away every handwriting of poverty, in the name of Jesus.

JANUARY 2016 POWER MUST CHANGE HANDS PRAYER POINTS

COMMAND THE YEAR

Praise worship

Scripture Reading - Psalm 91

Confession - Psalm 91

1. I take authority over this year, in the name of Jesus. I decree that all the elements of this year will cooperate with me. I decree that these elemental forces should refuse to cooperate with my enemies. I speak unto the sun, the moon and the stars. They must not smite me. I pull down every negative energy planning to operate against my life this year. This is the year the Lord has made, I will rejoice and be glad in it. I dismantle any power uttering incantations to capture this year. I render such incantations and satanic prayer null and void. I retrieve this year out of their hands, in the name of Jesus. Spirits of favour, counsel, might and power, come upon me, in the name of Jesus. I shall excel this year and nothing shall defile me. I shall possess the gates of my enemies.

2. The Lord shall anoint me with the oil of gladness above my fellows. The fire of the enemy shall not burn me. My ears shall hear good news and I shall not hear the voice of the enemy. My future is secured in Christ, in the name of Jesus. God has created me to do some definite services. He has committed into my hands some assignments which He has not committed to anybody. He has not created me for nothing. I shall do good. I shall do His work. I shall be an agent of peace. I will trust Him in whatever I do and wherever I am. I can never be thrown away or downgraded. There will be no poverty of body, soul and spirit in my life this year. The anointing of God upon my life gives me favour in the eyes of God and man all the days of my life. I shall not labour in vain. I shall walk this year in victory and liberty of the spirit.

3. This year, the Lord will make me a cheap winner and a candidate of uncommon testimonies, in the name of Jesus.

4. This year, I receive daily bread, good seed to sow every time, and

money to spend always, in the name of Jesus.

5. This year, my life will advertise the glory of God, in Jesus' name.

6. I cancel all appointments with sorrow, tragedy and evil cry this year, in the name of Jesus.

7. This year, I will encounter and experience a full scale laughter in all fronts, in the name of Jesus.

8. As from now on, blood-thirsty demons and robbers will flee at my presence, in the name of Jesus.

9. Whether I am on the sea, in the air or on the road, the evil forces there will bow to my authority, in the name of Jesus.

10. Anything I have waited for till now, for a long time, shall be miraculously delivered to me this year, in the name of Jesus.

11. My Father, make me and my family members completely immune to any form of sickness or disease this year, in the name of Jesus.

12. This year, I put myself and members of my family into the protective envelope of divine fire, in the name of Jesus.

13. This year, I will do the will of God and I will serve God, in the name of Jesus.

14. This year, I will have unconquerable victory, in Jesus' name.

15. This year, like a clay in the hands of the potter, the Lord will make what He wants out of my life, in the name of Jesus.

16. This year, the Lord will do with me whatever He wants, in the name of Jesus.

17. This year, the Lord will make me the head and not tail, in Jesus' name.

18. This year, every snare of the fowler assigned against me shall perish, in Jesus' name.

19. This year, I render the habitation of darkness assigned against me desolate, in the name of Jesus.

20. This year, divine deposits shall settle in my life, in the name of Jesus.

21. This year, I enter into the covenant of favour, in the name of Jesus.

22. This year, the anointing of success and fruitfulness shall rest on me, in the name of Jesus.

23. This year, I will not be a candidate of sweating without result, in Jesus' name.

24. This year, all obstacles on my way of progress shall be dismantled, in the name of Jesus.

25. This year, my God shall arise and my stubborn pursuers shall scatter, in Jesus' name.

26. This year, those who mock me in the past shall celebrate with me, in Jesus' name.

27. This year, my Goliath and Hamman shall experience destruction, in the name of Jesus.

28. This year, every power assigned to cut short my life shall die, in the name of Jesus.

29. This year, my prayers shall always provoke angelic violence for my good, in Jesus' name.

30. This year, I shall speak and my words shall bring testimonies, in the name of Jesus.

31. O thou that troubleth the Israel of Mountain of Fire and Miracles Ministries, the God of Elijah shall trouble you today.

32. Every enemy of the Mountain of Fire and Miracles Ministries, scatter, in the name of Jesus.

33. O God, arise and uproot anything You did not plant inside the Mountain of Fire and Miracles Ministries, in the name of Jesus.

34. Let the fire of revival fall upon Mountain of Fire and Miracles Ministries, in the name of Jesus.

www.ingramcontent.com/pod-product-compliance
Lightning Source LLC
Chambersburg PA
CBHW062115040426
42337CB00042B/3643